A fine group of Orders, Decorations and Medals. Awarded to Colonel J. D. Alexander, Royal Army Medical Corps. They include (top left to bottom right) the Commander's Neck Badge of the Order of the British Empire (CBE), the Distinguished Service Order (DSO), British campaign medals for India 1895–7, two for the Boer War 1899–1902 and three for 1914–18, and three foreign awards – the Belgian Order of Leopold, the Belgian Croix-de-Guerre and the French Croix-de-Guerre.

British Orders and D

Peter Duckers

D1310601

A Shire book

2

Published in 2004 by Shire Publications Ltd,
Cromwell House, Church Street, Princes Risborough,
Buckinghamshire HP27 9AA, UK.
(Website: www.shirebooks.co.uk)

Copyright © 2004 by Peter Duckers.
First published 2004.
Shire Album 424. ISBN 0 7478 0580 6.
Peter Duckers is hereby identified as the author of this
work in accordance with Section 77 of the Copyright,
Designs and Patents Act 1988.

British Library Cataloguing in Publication Data:
Duckers, Peter
British orders and decorations. – (Shire album; 424)
1. Orders of knighthood and chivalry – Great Britain –
History
2. Orders of knighthood and chivalry – Great Britain –
Insignia
I. Title
929.7'1'0941
ISBN 0 7478 0580 6

Cover: *The Breast Star of a Knight Commander of the Order of St Michael and St George. The enamelled
depiction of St Michael is surrounded by the motto of the Order, 'Auspicium melioris aevi' ('Token of a
better age').*

ACKNOWLEDGEMENTS
The author thanks the many recipients and collectors who have helped to assemble the
selection of photographs presented here or who have lent insignia for inclusion. He
particularly extends his thanks to the Trustees of the Shropshire Regimental Museum in
Shrewsbury Castle for permission to include insignia from the collection housed there, and
to Mr Derek Harrison, Mr Peter Fisher and Mr John Skingley for their assistance in
providing some of the insignia or images.

Printed in Great Britain by CIT Printing Services Ltd, Press Buildings,
Merlins Bridge, Haverfordwest, Pembrokeshire SA61 1XF

Contents

The origins of British Orders of Knighthood and Chivalry

This book examines the insignia associated with British Orders of Knighthood and related awards. In modern medallic terms, an 'Order' is a Badge that shows its wearer to be a member of a particular grade of an Order of Knighthood. Such Orders of Knighthood originated in medieval notions of chivalry and royal service and were established by all the ruling houses of Europe in the Middle Ages, though the origins of many are lost in the mists of time. Not surprisingly, the oldest European monarchies can boast the earliest examples of chivalric Orders – from the legendary French Order of the Holy Vial (said to date to AD 493) to the more reliably historical Portuguese Order of Aviz (1144), the Danish Order of Dannebrog (1219), the Polish Order of the White Eagle (1325) and the oldest surviving British example, the Order of the Garter, founded c.1348.

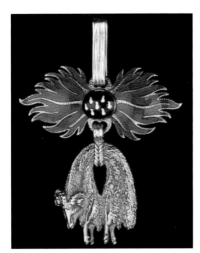

The secular Orders of Knighthood were essentially select 'brotherhoods' of noblemen, chosen by the monarch. They were bound to each other and to their sovereign not only by the usual feudal bonds but also by personal oath and, like their contemporaries the medieval religious Orders, by shared rituals and the observance of a strict code of conduct. Their members met regularly, in the Robes ascribed to their Order, usually in a dedicated Chapel, and observed the ceremonies and rites prescribed by their Statutes. In the Middle Ages, these aristocratic brotherhoods were a means of reinforcing the

Above: *The Order of the Golden Fleece (1429). Originally a Burgundian Order, it descended into both the Austrian and the Spanish branches of the Hapsburg family and was conferred by both houses only upon the highest ranks of the aristocracy and heads of state.*

Right: *The Russian Order of St Stanislas, second class. Instituted by the Polish monarchy in 1765, it was adopted as a Russian award when Poland came under Russian sway after partition in the late eighteenth century. It continued to be awarded until the fall of the Tsarist regime in 1917.*

A miniature medal group, comprising the Companion's Badge of the Order of St Michael and St George (CMG), the Member's Badge of the Royal Victorian Order (MVO), Medals for the Second World War and the 1953 Coronation Medal. Such miniatures are worn in place of full-sized versions on mess dress or in formal attire.

authority of the king, cementing loyalty to him amongst the higher echelons of his nobility and offering a prestigious reward (close association with the monarch and his patronage) to potentially dangerous warrior aristocrats. Members of foreign noble houses were also admitted as signal indications of royal favour or to cement military or family alliances.

As the Middle Ages waned and 'warrior aristocrats' gave way to a civilised peerage and to educated landed gentlemen, the military function of the Orders declined. Where they survived, it was as another way by which a monarch could show favour to high-ranking members of the aristocracy or (increasingly) as honours for distinguished service rendered to the sovereign and state. Indeed, the need to recognise such service has never declined and newer Orders have been established throughout the world in more recent times – by South American nations, which freed themselves from Spanish rule in the nineteenth century, by states (like the Ottoman Empire and Japan) seeking to emulate 'modern' Europe, and even by newly established post-imperial African and South-east Asian states. The value of establishing and conferring Orders – if only as actual Medals and Decorations, far removed from notions of Knighthood and Chivalry – continues to be recognised around the world; there are few modern states – Algeria, Burma and China being rare examples – that do *not* have a system of graded Orders with which to reward the services of their most distinguished citizens.

The appointment of a person to an Order is still seen as a valid means of honouring distinguished service, though Orders are now conferred along more democratic and meritorious lines to reflect the wide range of people from all walks of life who render outstanding service to their community or nation in every field of endeavour.

Below: The Order of Australia (1975). Even in our egalitarian times, modern states are not averse to the creation of Orders rewarding distinguished service. Many Commonwealth countries have established their own Orders or may nominate their citizens for British versions.

British Orders: general features

From the earliest times, the monarch has been 'the fount of honour' – the source of appointments to Orders and other state rewards. However, from the eighteenth century onwards, and increasingly as the progress of parliamentary democracy accelerated, the honours system was taken over by the governing political parties and most awards became a matter for the Prime Minister and the government. Nevertheless, despite the encroachment of politics into the honours system, the monarch maintains an important influence over appointments to the 'Great Orders' (see pages 15–20) and retains control not only over the more obviously personal 'royal' awards – such as the Royal Family Orders and the Royal Victorian Order – but also over the Order of Merit and the Companions of Honour. The monarch is also consulted over appointments to other Orders and has to give consent before they can be publicly announced.

New appointments are announced twice yearly in *The London Gazette* (an official government publication), in the New Year's Honours List in January and in the monarch's Birthday Honours in June. Supplementary lists may be published at other times as required – associated with royal visits overseas, state visits to the United Kingdom, special occasions or in times of war. It is customary, but not absolutely the rule, for the monarch to present the insignia of awards in person during formal investitures, this being especially true for the higher grades of all Orders. Where this is impossible (for example in times of

A page of 'The London Gazette' for December 1904, announcing appointments to the Royal Victorian Order. All appointments to Orders and the award of Decorations (for example for gallantry) are announced in this official government publication, which dates from 1665.

war) some may be publicly conferred locally by other dignitaries, such as Army commanders, the county Lord Lieutenant or the Mayor, or may even be sent through the post with no formal ceremony or procedure being observed.

Appointees receive an official Warrant or certificate of appointment, which is usually signed personally by the monarch, though on occasion, such as in wartime when there may be large numbers of awards, a secretarial signature or stamp may be used. The administration of the system – maintaining registers, conducting general correspondence, issuing Warrants and Statutes and sending or receiving insignia, among other duties – is undertaken by the Central Chancery of the Orders of Knighthood in St James's Palace, London.

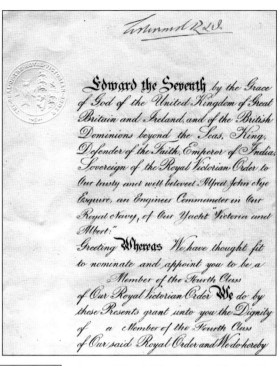

Above: *A Royal Warrant signed by the King, conferring the status of Member of the Royal Victorian Order (MVO) on a 'trusty and well-beloved' subject. Such documents employ formal and standardised forms of address that have been in use for generations.*

CENTRAL CHANCERY OF THE ORDERS OF KNIGHTHOOD
ST JAMES'S PALACE
OFFICES – 8, BUCKINGHAM GATE, S.W. 1.
TELEPHONE – VICTORIA 2837 & 2838

Reference 6/8/60   22nd October, 1960.

Sir,

    I acknowledge with thanks the receipt of the Badge of a Commander of the Military Division of the Most Excellent Order of the British Empire, returned by you consequent upon your promotion in the Order.

    I enclose herewith a formal receipt (No.3253) for the return of this Badge.

I am, Sir,

Your obedient servant.

Secretary.

Sir Duncan L. Anderson,
      K.B.E.,
c/o Federal Power Board,
P.O. Box 630,
Salisbury,
SOUTHERN RHODESIA.

Left: *Letter regarding the return of the Badge of a Commander of the Order of the British Empire on promotion to the higher grade of Knight Commander. It is usual for those promoted within an Order to return the insignia of the lower grade – since they cannot wear both.*

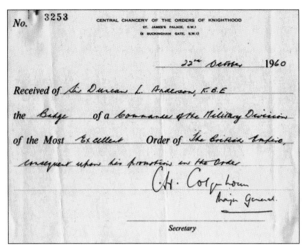

Receipt for the insignia of a Commander of the Order of the British Empire, returned by a recipient who had been promoted to Knight Commander. Such matters are administered by the Central Chancery of the Orders of Knighthood, based in St James's Palace, London.

The regulations and codes of conduct for each Order are laid down in its Statutes, which may be amended from time to time (for instance to allow for additional members or the appointment of ladies) by the authority of the sovereign. Newly appointed members receive a copy of the current Statutes of their Order.

It is possible under exceptional circumstances (such as the committing of treason) for a recipient to be 'degraded' and to forfeit an honour. The insignia are returned to the Central Chancery and the recipient's name is erased from the Register of the Order. In older times, such degradations were both highly public and humiliating.

The insignia of the Orders – the Collar Chains, Breast Stars, Neck Badges and Breast Badges – are presented in fitted cases, usually

with the Order and grade named on the lid. They contain instructions for wearing and identify the manufacturer of the piece. Although the Royal Mint undertakes the production of some insignia, there is a wide range of private manufacturers, most of them jewellers of established repute. In earlier times some recipients chose to have their insignia made to a personal specification; the result of this is that there is a wide variation in the quality and even in the dimensions of earlier awards and some pieces

The Statutes of the Order of the British Empire. The Statutes of any of the Orders may be revised or added to by the monarch from time to time as new circumstances require (for example to allow the admission of women to the Order).

INSTRUCTIONS FOR WEARING THE BADGE OF THE THIRD CLASS OF AN ORDER.
(*e.g.* **C.B., C.M.G., C.V.O., C.B.E.**)

The Badge of the Third Class of an Order should be worn in the following manner:—

(*a*) **When worn with Uniform.**—The Badge suspended from the riband of the Order (normal width) should be worn round the neck, inside and under the Collar of the Uniform Coat, in the manner described in the Dress Regulations of the Service to which the holder belongs, or belonged formerly.

(*b*) **When worn with Full Evening Dress (i.e., Tail Coat).**—The Badge (full size), suspended from the riband of the Order (preferably of Miniature width) should be worn round the neck under the white tie. The Badge should hang about one inch below the tie. At the same time, provided the holder of this Badge is in possession of one or more other Orders, Decorations or Medals, it is permissible to wear, with the miniatures of these, the miniature of this Badge also. Miniatures can be purchased from any Military Tailor and from most London Jewellers.

(*c*) **With Morning Dress (Civilian attire).**—On suitable occasions, at the discretion of the holder, the Badge may be worn round the neck under the tie, which should be a bow tie, in a manner similar to that in which it is worn with full evening dress.

In the event of promotion to a higher Class in the Order, the Badge should be returned to The Secretary, Central Chancery of the Orders of Knighthood (St. James's Palace), 8, Buckingham Gate, London, S.W.1.

The Badge is not returnable at death and may be retained by the relatives of the deceased who are requested to notify The Secretary, Central Chancery of the Orders of Knighthood, of the date of decease.

Above: *The card accompanying a 'Third Class Order' (Companion or Commander level), explaining how it should be worn. These cards are given with the box of issue of most awards.*

Left: *A case of issue: the box for the Breast Badge of an Officer of the Order of the British Empire (OBE), Military Division. Most British Orders are presented in a fitted case, with the Order and grade identified on the lid.*

A Breast Badge of a Member of the Order of the British Empire (MBE) in its fitted case of issue. This is the first type MBE, with the 'Seated Britannia' central design (1917–36) and the first type purple ribbon; the central scarlet stripe denotes an award in the Military Division. Note also the maker's details clearly displayed on the inner lid.

Examples of manufacturers' labels by the Royal Mint and Garrard & Co. The names of a wide range of other manufacturers and jewellers are to be found.

are of exquisite workmanship. Leading manufacturers of insignia in modern times include Toye, Kenning, Spencer; Spink & Son; Elkington; Storr & Mortimer; Collingwood and – perhaps the most frequently seen – Garrard & Co., the royal jewellers. Manufacturers are identified by their trade details on the inner lid of the case or by the hallmarks on the insignia themselves. Since most insignia (other than personal purchases) were returnable on the death of the recipient, pieces earlier than the late eighteenth century and many of the Badges of the Great Orders (the Garter, the Thistle and St Patrick) are rarely seen.

A highly jewelled 'private purchase' Breast Star of the Grand Cross of the Order of the Bath. Those who wished to commission or purchase much more elaborate versions of insignia were free to do so – at whatever price they cared to pay.

A cloth Breast Star of the Grand Cross of the Order of the Bath. Only cloth and bullion versions of Stars were officially issued before c.1852. Their rather poor quality led many recipients to purchase their own metal types – which explains the wide range of materials and quality to be found in the early Breast Stars of all Orders.

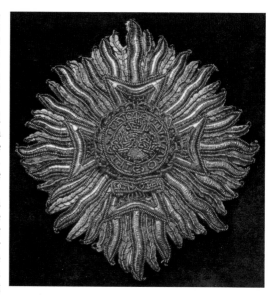

In contrast to some continental systems, for example Tsarist Russian awards, British Orders tend to be restricted to relatively few grades. The usual three (unless otherwise described below) are:

Knight or Dame Grand Cross. On formal occasions associated with the ceremonies of their Order, these wear the elaborate Robes and the Collar Chain with pendant Badge of the Order. Each Order has its own distinctive Robes, the Mantle bearing the embroidered Badge of the Order on the left shoulder. On other formal occasions they wear the Sash and Sash Badge with Breast Star. This grade confers the status of Knighthood or the title of Dame.

Knight or Dame Commander. Knights wear a Breast Star and a Neck Badge suspended from the ribbon of the Order, whilst Dames wear the equivalent of the Neck Badge on a bow of ribbon above the left breast. Until 1852 Breast Stars were awarded in cloth, bullion wire and sequins and were often of poor quality – which is why many recipients had their own metal Stars made and why so many differences in dimension, quality and design occur in earlier awards. This grade confers the status of Knighthood or the title of Dame.

The Collar Chain and pendant Badge of the Grand Cross of the Order of the Bath, Civil Division. The Chain is worked in gold, with nine crowns and eight enamelled 'devices' comprising a rose, shamrock and thistle issuing from a sceptre. These are joined by white enamelled knots.

King George V in Field Marshal's uniform. He wears Breast Stars of the Garter, the Star of India and the Bath, as well as the Royal Victorian Chain and the Neck Badge of the Bath. His Breast Badges (mounted in a row) are (left to right) the Orders of the Bath, the Star of India, St Michael and St George, the Indian Empire, the Royal Victorian Order, the Imperial Service Order and two foreign awards.

Companion or *Commander*. Initially, gentlemen wore the Badge of the Order (for example, CB, CMG or CIE) on a ribbon on the left breast, in the fashion of other Medals, but increasingly (after 1917 with some Orders) it became the practice to wear the Badge suspended around the neck from the ribbon of the Order. Ladies wear the Badge on a bow of the ribbon above the left breast. This grade does not confer the status of Knighthood or the title of Dame.

General Sir A. H. Bingley wearing the Neck and Breast Badges of a Knight Commander of the Order of the Indian Empire (KCIE), the Neck Badge of a Companion of the Order of the Bath (CB) and the Breast Badge of the Order of St John of Jerusalem. At the head of his row of awards he wears the Kaisar-i-Hind Medal.

Order of Precedence

Since some British Orders are accorded a higher status than others, they have an 'Order of Precedence', which is reflected in their wearer's position on formal, state or ceremonial occasions and in the position of the Badge of the Order when worn with other official awards. Throughout this book all the Orders are listed (within their respective chapters) according to their official Order of Precedence.

Below is the Order of Precedence for the higher grades of the Orders, with the full title of each Order, its date of institution and its motto.

The Most Noble Order of the Garter (1348)
Honi soit qui mal y pense ('Shame to him who thinks badly of it')

The Most Ancient and Most Noble Order of the Thistle (1687)
Nemo me impune lacessit ('No-one strikes me with impunity')
A reference to the thorns of the thistle, which has been used as an emblem of Scotland since at least the early sixteenth century.

The Most Illustrious Order of St Patrick (1783)
Quis separabit ('Who shall separate us?')
A reference to the unity of England and Ireland and the loyalty of the Irish peerage during the American Revolution. The political union was not formalised until the Act of Union in 1800.

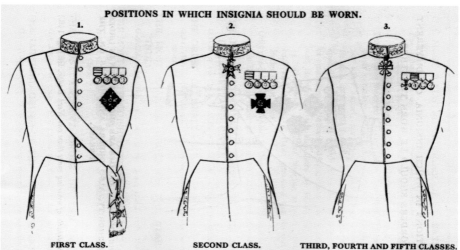

POSITIONS IN WHICH INSIGNIA SHOULD BE WORN.

1.   2.   3.

FIRST CLASS.   SECOND CLASS.   THIRD, FOURTH AND FIFTH CLASSES.

Sketches showing the Manner in which the Insignia of the Five Classes of an Order should be worn.

NOTE.— *In Diagram 3 the Third Class is the Neck Badge and the Fourth or Fifth Classes the Badge on the breast.*

Wearing positions for different grades of Orders in uniform. (Left to right) Sash and Breast Badge (Grand Cross level); Neck and Breast Badge (Knight Commander level); Neck Badge (Companion or Commander level); various Breast Badges (Officer, Lieutenant, Member level).

The Most Honourable Order of the Bath (1725)
Tria juncta in uno ('Three joined as one')
A reference to the union of England, Ireland and
Scotland and/or to the Holy Trinity.

The Order of Merit (1902)
No motto

The Baronet's Badge (1689/1926)
Fax mentis honestae gloria ('Renown is the torch of the
virtuous mind')

The Most Exalted Order of the Star of India (1861)
Heaven's light our guide

The Most Distinguished Order of St Michael and St George (1818)
Auspicium melioris aevi ('Token of a better age')

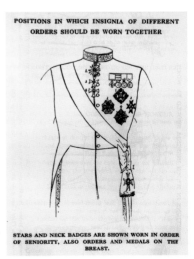

POSITIONS IN WHICH INSIGNIA OF DIFFERENT
ORDERS SHOULD BE WORN TOGETHER

STARS AND NECK BADGES ARE SHOWN WORN IN ORDER
OF SENIORITY, ALSO ORDERS AND MEDALS ON THE
BREAST.

The Most Eminent Order of the Indian Empire (1878)
The Badge initially bore the simple legend *Victoria Imperatrix*
('Victoria, Empress'), but following the queen's death in 1901 it was
altered to *Imperatricis auspiciis* ('Under the auspices of the Empress').

*Above: The order of
wear: multiple
awards of Orders are
worn in a set fashion,
according to their
Order of Precedence,
as illustrated in this
diagram of 1937.*

The Imperial Order of the Crown of India (1878)
No motto

The Royal Victorian Order (1896)
No motto

The Order of the Companions of Honour (1917)
In action faithful and in honour clear

The Most Excellent Order of the British Empire (1917)
For God and the Empire

The Imperial Service Order (1902)
No motto

The Order of St John of Jerusalem (1888)
No motto

*Formal Robes of the Order of the Thistle (left) and the Order of St
Patrick (right). These robes with the Collar and pendant Badge of the
Order are worn by Knights or Dames Grand Cross only on the most
formal occasions actually associated with the rituals of the Order.
On other occasions they wear the Sash, Sash Badge and Breast Star.*

The 'Great Orders'

The three earliest and most prestigious British Orders of Knighthood – the Garter, the Thistle and St Patrick – are known as the 'Great Orders'.

The Order of the Garter (1348)

The establishment of the most senior British Order can be dated to the 1340s, though there is no agreement on the actual foundation year. The year 1348 – in which the Order's Chapel of St George was consecrated in Windsor Castle – is usually taken as the date of foundation, though there are grounds for thinking that it may have been established slightly earlier, possibly in 1344. King Edward III, then at the outset of the Hundred Years' War against France, seems to have intended to recreate the spirit of the Arthurian Knights of the Round Table, at that time widely considered to be historical fact. Edward clearly wished to create a powerful brotherhood that would serve him faithfully in times of war. The supposed origins of the strange title of the Order are familiar: at a formal function, King Edward is said to have picked up the fallen garter of Joan, Countess of Salisbury, and to spare her blushes fastened it on to his own leg with the comment '*Honi soit qui mal y pense*' ('Shame to him who thinks badly of it'). But this is no doubt a myth and the Garter may symbolise simply a bond or unifying feature amongst the military brotherhood established by Edward. The motto may refer to criticism of Edward's claim to the throne of France.

The Order initially comprised the Sovereign, the Prince of Wales and twenty-four Knights, all veterans of the French campaigns. It was enlarged by George III and William IV, long after its military function had

The insignia of the Order of the Garter.

The Garter: dark blue velvet, with the motto of the Order ('Honi soit qui mal y pense') embroidered or picked out in gold thread. Elaborate presentation versions or privately commissioned types are known, for example with the wording decorated with diamonds.

The 'Lesser George': the Sash Badge of the Order of the Garter. A plain gold type is shown against the background of the Sash. As with many other early Badges of British Orders, there is a wide variety of styles, materials and even dimensions in such insignia as many recipients chose to have their own personalised version.

ceased, to admit the lineal descendants of George I in addition to the twenty-six members of the original foundation. Somewhat unusually, ladies were admitted from its earliest days, though in an 'honorary' capacity in what was a military association. The last such appointment in the Middle Ages was that of Margaret Beaufort, mother of King Henry VII. After her death in 1509 the admission of ladies fell into abeyance until revived by Edward VII in 1901, when Queen Alexandra was appointed. However, it was not until 1987 that ladies were *formally* admitted to the Order, an example being Baroness Thatcher. Foreign members, often heads of state or of ruling families, may also be admitted as 'extra' Knights and are known as 'Stranger Knights'.

There is only one class (with male and female equivalents), Knight (KG) or Lady (LG) of the Garter. The Robes are of dark blue velvet lined with white satin, with the Badge of the Order on the left shoulder. The Hood is black velvet and the Bonnet red velvet with ostrich plumes. The Sash is dark blue, 100 mm (3.9 inches) wide and worn over

An early-nineteenth-century silver Breast Star of the Order of the Garter. Note the loops to facilitate sewing the Star on to a jacket.

The formal Robes of the Order of the Garter, here worn by Edward, Prince of Wales, the future Edward VIII. Knights wear the actual Garter around the leg, below the left knee, and Ladies wear it above the left elbow.

the left shoulder.

Appointments remain 'in the gift' of the monarch, with new appointments announced on 23rd April (St George's Day). Knights are invested by the monarch in person in formal ceremonies in St George's Chapel during the Order's gathering in Windsor Castle each June.

The Collar Chain of the Order of the Garter, with pendant Badge (the 'George') featuring the patron saint of England and of the Order, St George, in a familiar pose. The 'George' here is an elaborate coloured enamel version.

The magnificent Chapel of the Order of St George in Windsor Castle. It has been the spiritual home and meeting place of the Order since its consecration especially for this purpose in 1348.

The insignia of the Order of the Thistle.

The Order of the Thistle (1687)

Scotland's senior Order – its equivalent of the Garter – was formally instituted in May 1687. However, the thistle was adopted as a Scottish royal emblem by James III as far back as the early sixteenth century and an Order 'of the Thissill' was conferred by James V on the French king Francis I in 1535. Some believe that its lineage may be traced to an Order of St Andrew dating to AD 787 or 809 – which would make it senior to the Garter by several centuries!

The foundation of 1687 comprised the Sovereign and twelve Knights, the total number alluding to Christ and His Apostles, but fell into abeyance with the downfall of the Stuart family in the 'Glorious Revolution' of 1688. The Order was revived by Queen Anne in 1703 and modified in subsequent revisions to its Statutes. The number of Knights was increased to sixteen in 1827 and Queen Victoria allowed for additional appointments to members of her family. The Knights have generally been the most senior of the Scottish nobility, members of the royal family and people of Scottish descent who have rendered outstanding service to Scotland or to Great Britain, often in the higher ranks of government. Only since 1987 have ladies been eligible, the Princess Royal being appointed in June 2001. There is only one grade to the Order, that of Knight (KT) or Lady (LT) of the Thistle.

The Robes are in green velvet with a purple Hood, the Badge of the Order borne on the left shoulder. The

The Collar Chain and Badge of the Grand Cross of the Order of the Thistle. The Chain is in gold, with alternate links of enamelled thistles and sprigs of rue.

Bonnet is black velvet with ostrich plumes. The Sash is dark green, 100 mm (3.9 inches) wide and worn over the left shoulder.

The Chapel, originally intended in 1687 for Holyrood Palace, was established only in 1911, in St Giles's Cathedral, Edinburgh.

The Order of St Patrick (1783)

The most senior Irish Order was established by George III on 5th February 1783. It was intended to reward members of the Irish peerage for their loyalty during the American Revolution (1776–83) and to strengthen the bonds of unity between the Crown and the Irish aristocracy. It originally comprised the Sovereign and fifteen Knights but was extended in 1833 to include the Lord Lieutenant of Ireland (as Grand Master of the Order) and twenty-two Knights. As is usual with British Orders, the Statutes allowed for the appointment of honorary and foreign Knights. Its members were usually derived from the royal family and the highest-ranking Irish nobility.

There was only one grade to the Order, that of Knight (KP). The Robes were sky blue silk with the Badge of the Order on the left shoulder. The Sash was sky blue, 100 mm (3.9 inches) wide, worn over the right shoulder (not over the left as with the other Great Orders) and bore the Badge over the right hip.

The insignia of the Order of St Patrick.

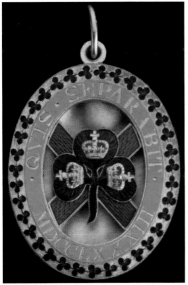

The Sash Badge of the Order of St Patrick in gold and enamels. The Sash Badge is a saltire cross in red enamel, surmounted by a green shamrock with gold crowns superimposed. The surround is on blue enamel, bearing the motto of the Order and its foundation date in gold. A band of thirty-two shamrocks surrounds the whole Badge.

The silver Breast Star of the Order of St Patrick. It bears an enamelled shamrock in the centre, surrounded by the motto of the Order, 'Quis separabit', and the date of institution, 1783, in Latin numerals.

The Chapel was originally in St Patrick's Cathedral, Dublin, but the Order was secularised in 1871. Appointments to the Order ceased with the partition of Ireland in 1922 and the establishment of the Irish Free State; it has been obsolete since the death of its last holder, Prince Henry, Duke of Gloucester, in 1974.

Field Marshal the Duke of Connaught, wearing a fine array of Breast Stars – the Orders of the Bath, the Garter, St Michael and St George and St John of Jerusalem. He wears the Sash and Badge of the Order of the Garter.

Other British Orders

The Order of the Bath (1725)

Some form of 'Order of the Bath' can be traced back to *c*.1399, its unusual title deriving from medieval ceremonies of knighthood. Before installation as a Knight, the candidate undertook a ritual bath, reminiscent of the rite of baptism, as a symbol of purification. There is archival reference to this ceremony as early as 1128. The Order had all but fallen into abeyance by the end of the seventeenth century but was revived in 1725 by King George I as a new single-class military Order, which would comprise the monarch and thirty-seven Knights (KB).

A section of the Collar or Chain of the Grand Cross of the Order of the Bath.

During the eighteenth century, the Bath became for the King and his leading politicians a way of bestowing a sign of royal favour upon prominent aristocrats – as much to retain their support as for any achievement – with the 'military' nature of the Order becoming more pronounced as the century progressed and Britain became involved in a series of major wars. Thereafter, the Order was usually

A Breast Star of a Knight Commander of the Order of the Bath in sequins and bullion thread – typical of the type of Star officially issued before 1852, in which year solid metal versions (usually silver) were conferred.

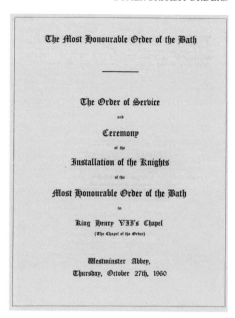

The Most Honourable Order of the Bath

The Order of Service
and
Ceremony
of the
Installation of the Knights
of the
Most Honourable Order of the Bath
in
King Henry VII's Chapel
(The Chapel of the Order)

Westminster Abbey,
Thursday, October 27th, 1960

Above: *The magnificent Henry VII Chapel in Westminster Abbey, showing the stalls of the Knights of the Bath with the banners of the Knights Grand Cross hanging above them.*

Right: *A programme for the installation of new Knights of the Bath in the Henry VII Chapel, Westminster Abbey, in 1960.*

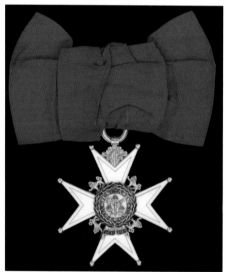

The Sash and Badge of a Knight Grand Cross of the Bath, Military Division.

A Breast Star in gold and silver of a Knight Grand Cross of the Bath, Military Division.

conferred upon senior military and naval commanders, such as the Duke of Wellington and Lord Nelson.

From the outset, the Chapel of the Order was the beautiful Henry VII Chapel in Westminster Abbey and until 1812 each Knight had his own named stall with his personal banner and arms hung above. This practice was discontinued between 1812 and 1913 but since then the more senior Knights have had a named stall in the Chapel. Foreigners may be appointed as honorary members (an example being Ronald Reagan,

Left: *The Neck Badge of a Knight Commander of the Order of the Bath, Civil Division, c.1885. The central design features the triple-crown motif of the Order of the Bath with emblems of England, Scotland and Ireland.*

Right: *A fine example of the Companion's Neck Badge in gold of the Order of the Bath, Civil Division, c.1885. Note the slight design differences between this badge and the Knight Commander's Badge (left).*

ex-President of the United States) but ladies were admitted only in 1971. Every four years the members attend a formal service, with new installations taking place as required, and every eight years the monarch attends the service in person.

The Robes are of crimson satin lined with white taffeta. The Star of the Grand Cross is embroidered on the left shoulder. The high-crowned Hat is of black velvet, with a plume of white ostrich feathers. The Sash is plain dark red, carrying the Badge of the Order over the right hip.

After the French wars of 1793–1815 it was felt that some means should be found to reward officers who had rendered distinguished service in campaigns across the globe. It was decided therefore to remodel the Order to extend it to three grades, which are now Knight or Dame Grand Cross (GCB), Knight or Dame Commander (KCB/DCB) and Companion (CB). A Civil Division of only one class, Knight Grand Cross, was also established in 1815 but in 1847 this was brought into line with the Military Division and extended to three classes. Unusually in the series of British Orders, Civil and Military Divisions each have very different insignia. In modern times the Statutes allow, in addition to the Sovereign and the Great Master (the Prince of Wales in 2004), for 120 GCBs, 295 KCBs or DCBs and 1455 CBs. These numbers may be increased in exceptional circumstances.

General Sir John McQueen (1836-1909), one of the most famous 'frontier fighters' of the Indian Army. He wears the Sash and Brest Star of the Military GCB, conferred in 1889.

The Collar and pendant Badge of the Grand Cross of the Civil Division (far left) and Military Division (near left) of the Order of the Bath as depicted in the Statutes of the Order. Unusually, there are significant differences in the insignia of the Military and Civil Divisions – as is apparent in these illustrations.

Left: *The Companion's Breast Badge of the Order of the Bath, Military Division, in gold, pre-1887. Note its usual decorative gold buckle. The Badge was made in silver-gilt after 1887 and worn suspended around the neck after 1917.*

The Military Division of the Bath – especially at Companion level – soon became a form of long-service award, granted to high-ranking officers on retirement and only rarely for distinguished service on campaign. Its Civil version was granted to civil servants and politicians, equally for long and distinguished service, in the same way that the Order of St Michael and St George became a reward for imperial and overseas administrative service.

The Companion's Neck Badge of the Order of the Bath, Military Division, in silver-gilt. The Badges of the Military Division are much more ornate than the plain gold types of the Civil Division.

The Order of Merit, 1902. The only piece of insignia associated with this prestigious award is the Neck Badge, with civil or military versions. It carries the cypher of the reigning monarch on the obverse centre and the words 'For Merit' on the reverse.
The badge of the Military Division (right) is distinguished by the crossed swords through the centre.

The Order of Merit (1902)

Founded by Edward VII in 1902, the Order of Merit is a special distinction 'given to such persons ... as may have rendered exceptionally meritorious service in Our Crown Services or towards the advancement of the Arts, Learning, Literature and Science or such other exceptional service'.

The Order remains in the gift of the Sovereign and is restricted to twenty-four members as well as additional foreign recipients (who have included Mother Teresa and Nelson Mandela). There is a Military Division included in the membership of twenty-four, Lord Louis Mountbatten being one such recipient.

Past British holders of this very select Order have included some of the most distinguished contributors to British culture, science and industry: Florence Nightingale, Augustus John, Henry Moore, Sir Edward Elgar, Ralph Vaughan Williams, Benjamin Britten, Thomas Hardy, T. S. Eliot, E. M. Forster, Bertrand Russell, former prime ministers Sir Winston Churchill and Earl Attlee, General Baden-Powell (founder of the Boy Scouts), Field Marshals Haig and Kitchener, and Admirals Jellicoe and Beatty.

Formal Robes. (Left) The Grand Cross of the Star of India, worn by a Field Marshal. (Centre) The Grand Cross of the Order of the Bath, worn by an Admiral. (Right) A Grand Cross of the Order of St Michael and St George, worn by a diplomat in court dress.

The Sash and Sash Badge of the Grand Cross of the Order of St Michael and St George.

The Order of St Michael and St George (1818)

On the conclusion of the French wars in 1815, the island of Malta and the Ionian Islands in the Adriatic were ceded to Great Britain as naval and military bases to support British interests in the Mediterranean. The Order of St Michael and St George was instituted on 27th April 1818 by the Prince Regent (who became King George IV in 1820) to reward the services of the inhabitants of these possessions. Although the Ionian Islands were transferred to Greece in 1859, the Order was retained and increasingly became a reward for long and/or distinguished service in the colonies and other imperial territories.

The Order has been widely awarded to colonial administrators and to ambassadors, diplomats and civil servants or to those who rendered distinguished service in Britain's overseas possessions. Ladies became eligible for the award only in 1965. The Order is restricted to 125 Knights or Dames Grand Cross (GCMG), 375 Knight or Dame Commanders (KCMG/DCMG) and

Below left: *The Breast Star of the Grand Cross of the Order of St Michael and St George. Its central roundel features an enamelled depiction of St Michael surrounded by the motto of the Order, 'Auspicium melioris aevi'.*

Below right: *Reverse of a Breast Star (in this case, of a Knight Grand Cross of the Order of St Michael and St George), showing the vertical pin – a fastening standard to most British Stars – that attaches the emblem to the jacket or dress.*

Left: *The Neck Badge of a Companion of the Order of St Michael and St George. Insignia of this grade were worn as Breast Badges until 1917 and afterwards around the neck.*

Below: *A high-quality Breast Star of a Knight Commander of the Order of St Michael and St George. Note the difference in design to the Star of the Grand Cross (opposite).*

1750 Companions (CMG). As usual, foreigners may be appointed as honorary members. Until 1864 the Order's ceremonies were held in Corfu, but since 1904 its Chapel has been in St Paul's Cathedral.

The Robes comprise a Mantle of Saxon blue lined with scarlet silk with the Badge of the Order on the left shoulder. The Hat is of blue satin, lined with scarlet and carrying black and white ostrich feathers. The Sash is a broad ribbon of the Order, worn over the right shoulder and bearing the Badge over the right hip.

The Order of the Star of India (1861)

After the trauma of the Indian Mutiny of 1857–8 the powers of the East India Company were removed and the government of the Indian Empire passed to the Crown and to London.

The magnificent Order of the Star of India was instituted in 1861, initially to reward Indian princes and others who had rendered loyal service during the Mutiny. It later became a reward for long and

The Order of the Star of India – the Companion's Neck Badge in a Garrard case of issue. The Badge was worn on the breast until 1917 and then around the neck, to bring it into line with the practice of other awards of this grade.

Far left: *The Companion's Badge of the Star of India, obverse, showing the individually hand-cut cameo portrait of the founder, Queen Victoria, surrounded by the motto of the Order, 'Heaven's light our guide', set in diamonds on a blue enamel background.*

Left: *The plain reverse of the Companion's Badge of the Star of India, showing the gold base and dark red enamel backing for the cameo of Queen Victoria.*

distinguished service within the Indian Empire. It continued to be awarded to Indian princely rulers as a mark of favour but many of the lower grades were conferred upon civil servants, judges and other administrators, and occasionally upon military officers – though not usually for war service. There was no distinction in the insignia or ribbons for civil or military service.

As with other British-Indian awards, the Order became obsolete when India gained independence in 1947.

The magnificent Breast Star of a Knight Grand Commander of the Order of the Star of India. That of a Knight Commander is in silver, not gold.

The Breast Star of a Knight Commander of the Order of the Indian Empire.

The Order of the Indian Empire (1877)

In 1876, to promote closer links between the monarch and her Indian subjects, the Royal Titles Act proclaimed that Queen Victoria would adopt the title 'Empress of India'. The new title was announced in Delhi in January 1877 and henceforth coins and medals bearing the official titles of the queen would carry the new 'style'. Her successors as kings of England would also be 'Emperor of India'.

The Order of the Indian Empire, instituted by Royal Warrant on 31st December 1877, is another reflection of the desire for closer links between the British monarchy and India. Initially – and unusually – there was to be only one class, Companion, the Badge to be worn on the breast. In August 1886 the Order was enlarged to two classes, adding the grade Knight Commander, and on 1st June 1887 it was extended to the usual three classes – Knight Grand Commander (GCIE), Knight Commander (KCIE) and Companion (CIE). The intention was to restrict the number of GCIE holders to twenty-five and KCIE holders to fifty, but with no limit on the number of Companions. The Order, which was to reward meritorious service within the Indian Empire, came to be regarded as a junior grade of the Order of the Star of India and was granted to civil and military recipients, though there is no difference in their insignia. Many of the higher grades went to senior officials of the Indian Civil Service ('the Heaven-born') and to members of the Indian princely families.

The attractive design of the Badge in the form of a

The later badge of a Companion of the Order of the Indian Empire. Soon irreverently known as the 'jam tart', it was reduced in diameter in 1877 and lost the lettering on the petals. As with other Orders at this grade, it was worn around the neck after 1917. The ribbon is plain 'imperial purple'.

Above: *The Companion's Badge of the Order of the Indian Empire, first type. The earlier Badges, before 1877, were larger than later types and had the letters 'I-N-D-I-A' on the petals.*

A group of dress miniatures showing the military CB and the CMG, the British War Medal for 1914–18, the 1935 Jubilee and 1937 Coronation Medals and the Volunteer Decoration for India.

Above: *The Collar Chain and pendant Badge of the Grand Cross of the Order of the British Empire, second type. Introduced in 1936, this type featured the conjoined portraits of the founders, King George V and Queen Mary. The ribbon was altered from plain purple (with a scarlet central stripe for the Military Division) to rose pink with pearl-grey edges (with a grey central stripe for the Military Division).*

red rose was chosen to avoid religious symbolism, given the wide range of religions within the Indian Empire whose members might be potential recipients. For the same reason, the title of the highest rank was Knight Grand Commander, not (as was customary in British Orders) Knight Grand Cross, to make this grade of the Order acceptable to non-Christian recipients such as Hindus, Muslims and Sikhs.

The Order was rendered obsolete in 1947 when India became independent.

The Order of the British Empire (1917)

Established in June 1917, this most recent of British Orders was born out of the conditions of the First World War. Although new military awards had been created to reflect the needs of the fighting services (such awards including the Military Cross and the Military Medal), it was felt that the efforts of a wider range of people needed to be recognised. Suggestions that existing Orders – such as the Bath or St Michael and St George – should be extended with the addition of new grades or the appointment of larger numbers were rejected in favour of a completely new Order.

The war effort had drawn in civilians, men and women, of every rank and status throughout the British Empire on a scale never before seen. Nursing, ordnance production, charitable work, transport, industry and recruitment were just some of the many vital civil activities deemed worthy of formal acknowledgement. It was also considered necessary to reward those in the military who were working 'behind the lines', for

The silver Breast Star of a Knight or Dame Grand Cross of the Order of the British Empire, second type.

The Breast Star of a Knight or Dame Commander of the Order of the British Empire, second type.

example in administration, in training camps or hospitals, or with prisoners of war. From the start, the Order was available to imperial recipients, to foreigners who had materially aided the British cause and to women whose work in many areas had been of crucial value to the war effort. It continued in use after the war as a reward for distinguished service to Britain and to Commonwealth countries in the arts, science, literature, administration, social work, charitable work, education and many other fields.

Although very much a creation of the modern world, and certainly the most widely awarded British Order, its regalia follow the traditional pattern – though it has five classes instead of the usual three. These are: Knight or Dame Grand Cross (GBE); Knight or Dame Commander (KBE/DBE); Commander (CBE); Officer of the Order (OBE); and Member of the Order (MBE). The Order has both a Military and a Civil Division but there is no difference in the insignia for these, with only the ribbon indicating which Division has been conferred.

The Robes originally comprised a Mantle of purple satin lined with white silk but this was altered, in the 1936 remodelling of the Order, to rose-pink satin lined with pearl-grey silk. The Badge of the Grand Cross is embroidered on the left shoulder. The Sash, a broad 96 mm (3.7 inch) wide ribbon of the Order, passes over the right shoulder and carries the Badge of the Order over the left hip. Dames wear a bow of the ribbon bearing a smaller Badge on the left shoulder. All insignia of the higher grades are returnable on the death of the holder and the lower ones on promotion to a higher grade.

The silver Member's Badge of the Order of the British Empire, Military Division, second type. Only the central grey stripe denotes that this is an award in the Military Division. The Officer's Badge is the same as this, but in gilt.

The cased Medal of the Order of the British Empire, Military Division, first type. This small medal, issued unnamed, was awarded only between 1917 and 1922, when it was replaced by the second type. Approximately two thousand were awarded.

The Neck Badge of a Commander of the Order of the British Empire (CBE), first type, Military Division. This bears the original 'Seated Britannia' central motif, altered in 1936 and the original purple and scarlet ribbon.

The original ribbon of 1917 was plain purple, with a narrow central stripe of scarlet introduced for the Military Division in 1918. In 1936 the ribbon was altered to pink with narrow edge-stripes of pearl grey, those awarded for military service having an additional central pearl-grey stripe. The original 'Seated Britannia' obverse design of the insignia was altered in 1936 to show the conjoined busts of King George V and Queen Mary as founders of the Order.

The Chapel of the Order, dedicated in 1969, is in the crypt of St Paul's Cathedral. Once every four years services are held for recipients of the Order, with around two thousand in attendance.

Apart from the five grades of the Order itself, a lower tier existed in the form of the Medal of the Order, commonly known as the British Empire Medal (BEM). The original small silver Medal was awarded for the same sort of work as was the Order, but at a lower level. From 1917 to 1922 it bore on its obverse the 'Seated Britannia' design used on the Badges of

The Neck Badge of a Commander of the Order of the British Empire, second type, showing portraits of King George V and Queen Mary as founders.

Above left: *The British Empire Medal, second type, obverse, Military Division. The BEM is unusual in that it does not show the effigy and titles of the monarch. When awarded for gallantry, the ribbon bore an emblem of crossed oak-leaves in silver. This was introduced in 1957 and discontinued in 1974 with the creation of the Queen's Gallantry Medal.*

Above right: *The British Empire Medal, second type, reverse. This has the ribbon of the Military Division, denoted by the additional central grey stripe, which is absent in the Civil version.*

The central roundel with the 'Seated Britannia' design used on all the insignia of the Order of the British Empire until 1936 and on the Medal of the Order until 1922.

the Order. After 1922 the Medal was enlarged and the design altered. It was established in two types, with the reverse wording 'For Meritorious Service' or 'For Gallantry', the latter type being known as the Empire Gallantry Medal (EGM). The EGM ceased to be awarded after 1940, when the George Cross was introduced, and the award of the BEM itself for any form of gallantry ceased in 1974 with the introduction of the Queen's Gallantry Medal. The Meritorious Service BEM was retained as a lower rank of the Order of the British Empire, but following John Major's reform of honours in 1993 it began to be phased out.

The Baronet's Badge (1629)

Baronets take precedence over all Knights, except those of the Order of the Garter. The first Baronets of England were created in May 1611 by James VI and I, who levied a fee of £1095 for the title, ostensibly for the settlement of Ulster (hence the prominence of the 'Red Hand' of Ulster in the later Badges). In reality, it was another means by which an impoverished Crown could raise money – in this case from the fees for the appointments and titles – without recourse to Parliament and the restraints it might impose. Baronets of Ireland were created in September 1619 and Baronets of Scotland in 1624, when land grants in Nova Scotia, Canada, were given to certain Scottish gentlemen 'as a means of promoting the

Above: The elaborate Baronet's Badge, first type, introduced by Charles I in 1629 and worn by Scottish Baronets to whom landed estates in Nova Scotia had been granted by James VI and I in 1624.

Below: The post-1928 Baronet's Badge, featuring very prominently the 'Red Hand' of Ulster, surrounded by a fretted gold band of roses, shamrocks and thistles, symbolising the United Kingdom.

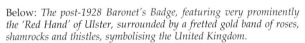

Above: The reverse of the modern Baronet's Badge: plain except for the recipient's title (in this case 'Williams of Park') and the date of appointment ('1928').

Sir Robert Williams of Park, Aberdeen. A colleague of Cecil Rhodes, he played a leading role in mining and railway development in Rhodesia and central Africa. For these services, he was appointed Baronet in 1928. He wears, in addition to the Baronet's Badge (immediately below the Collar), a Belgian and a Portuguese Order.

"plantation" of that province' (according to the original Statutes). These landed gentlemen were given the title Baronet of Nova Scotia and of Scotland in 1625. In 1629 they alone were allowed to wear a distinctive Baronet's Badge, with the Lion of Scotland prominently displayed.

After the union of England and Scotland in 1707, separate Scottish appointments ceased and new appointments were known as Baronets of Great Britain; after the union with Ireland in 1800, new appointments were Baronets of the United Kingdom. None of these wore a distinctive Badge.

Requests for the creation of a special Badge for *all* holders of the rank were increasingly made from the 1830s, but only in 1929, on the tercentenary of the original creation, was a standardised Baronet's Badge introduced. It displays the 'Red Hand' of Ulster on an enamel ground, with a fretted gold surround of roses, shamrocks and thistles. The reverse is plain except for the name of the recipient and the year of his appointment as Baronet. Appointments are made for distinguished service to the state.

The Knight Bachelor's Badge (1926)

In medieval times, Knights Bachelor were men knighted on the battlefield (as 'batteliers') for their services in combat. The rank, the

lowest grade of knighthood, can be traced back to the thirteenth century. Later, appointments were simply made as rewards for distinguished service to the state, the title being non-hereditary. However, although recipients were actually 'dubbed' with a sword by the sovereign, they wore no distinctive insignia until 1926. In that year, a gold Breast Badge was instituted by George V in response to a request from the Imperial Society of Knights Bachelor for a distinctive emblem to denote their rank.

Since 1973 the Badge has been worn around the neck on a red and white ribbon, although some recipients still prefer to wear the original Breast Badge.

The Knight Bachelor's Badge, first type, 81 mm (3.2 inches) long, in its fitted case of issue. It has the standard pin-back fitting (see page 26). The Badge's overall size was reduced in 1933 and again in 1973.

A modern Knight Bachelor's Badge; since 1973 these have been worn as a Neck Badge from a red and white ribbon. The sword, belt and spurs in the design reflect the origin of the title on the field of battle in the Middle Ages.

The Badge of the Order of Companions of Honour (1917)

The rank of Companion of Honour was instituted in June 1917 at the same time as the Order of the British Empire. Its Statutes specify that recipients must have 'rendered conspicuous service of national importance' and, as is common with British Orders, allow for the appointment of foreign dignitaries as honorary members.

Although the Order of Companions of Honour confers no title or precedence, it is very highly regarded and is conferred only on those who have rendered outstanding service to Great Britain or to Commonwealth countries. In many respects, it represents a 'lower tier' of the Order of Merit. Initially the Order comprised no more than fifty men and women but in 1963 the membership was increased to sixty-five, allocated as follows: forty-five for the United Kingdom, seven for Australia, two for New Zealand and eleven for other Commonwealth countries. The Order can be conferred for service of national importance, for example in the arts, literature, music, science, politics or industry. Famous recipients have included Sir Winston Churchill, Sir Michael Tippett (both of whom also held the Order of Merit), Dame Ninette de Valois, Canadian premier Pierre Trudeau, Sir John Gielgud, Dame Janet Baker, Lucian Freud and Professor Stephen Hawking.

The silver-gilt Badge is worn around the neck by men and from a bow of ribbon at the left shoulder by ladies. The ribbon is carmine red, edged with gold thread.

The Neck Badge of a Companion of Honour. As with the Order of Merit, there is only one piece of insignia – this Badge – though ladies wear it on a bow of the ribbon above the left breast, not around the neck. The reverse simply bears the cypher of the reigning monarch.

The Royal Family Orders

Apart from the range of national honours, many of which are controlled or influenced by the sovereign, there are five more personal awards that were or are entirely within the gift of the monarch. Three of these were or are awarded only to ladies.

The Royal Family Order (1820)

The custom of giving the royal portrait in miniature to wear as an Order was begun by George IV in 1820. Since then each monarch has conferred his or her own Royal Family Order, although Queen Victoria adopted a different type, in the form of the Royal Order of Victoria and Albert.

Possibly the most exclusive of all honours, the Royal Family Order is worn only by the queen and by female relatives of the sovereign. The award remains a private family affair, conferred informally.

The Badge consists of a miniature portrait of the reigning monarch within a surround of diamonds and is worn from a bow at the left shoulder. Formal photographs and portraits of the late Queen Mother frequently showed her wearing the Royal Family Order of her husband, King George VI, and of her daughter Queen Elizabeth II.

The Royal Family Order of King George VI. The reverse of these elaborate jewels bears the monarch's cypher.

The Royal Order of Victoria and Albert (1862)

This very personal Order, in four classes, was instituted by Queen Victoria on 10th February 1862 and was her own version of the Royal Family Order. It was awarded only to princesses 'of the Royal Blood' and other ladies and granted as a mark of personal favour. The Order was to comprise no more than forty-five holders in addition to the Queen. The First Class and Second Class were awarded solely to female members of the British and foreign royal families, whilst the Third and Fourth Classes were conferred upon ladies of the highest status, often members of the royal household.

The Badge of the first three classes was an onyx cameo conjoined portrait of Queen Victoria and Prince Albert, surmounted by a crown. The First and Second Classes were set in diamonds (the Second Class being smaller in size), the Third Class in pearls and diamonds. The Fourth

The Royal Order of Victoria and Albert. Effectively Queen Victoria's own personal version of the Royal Family Order, the Badge that she actually wore reversed this central design and had Prince Albert's head to the fore.

Queen Mary, consort of King George V. In this card of 1914 she wears the Royal Family Orders of Edward VII and George V and (below them) the Royal Order of Victoria and Albert. Also visible are the Garter – worn by ladies above the left elbow – and the Breast Star of the Garter.

Class was of a different design – the monogram 'V&A' set in pearls and rubies and surmounted by a crown. All were worn on the left shoulder from a bow of white moiré ribbon.

This Order was not conferred after the death of Queen Victoria in 1901. Its last holder, Princess Alice, Countess of Athlone, lived until 1981.

The Imperial Order of the Crown of India (1878)

Instituted on 1st January 1878 following Queen Victoria's assumption of the title 'Empress of India' in 1877, this Order was another reflection of the desire to link the British monarchy more closely with its Indian subjects (see also the Order of the Star of India and the Order of the Indian Empire [pages 27-30]).

It was conferred only upon ladies, British and Indian, who had rendered distinguished service of benefit to India. Some were conferred, for example, upon ladies of the Indian princely families for charitable or social work over a long period.

The beautiful Badge consisted of the royal cipher, VRI (*Victoria Regina et Imperatrix,* 'Victoria, Queen and Empress'), in diamonds, pearls and turquoises, encircled by a band of pearls, surmounted by the Imperial Crown in jewels and enamels. It was worn from a bow of light blue ribbon with white edges. As with other Indian Orders, it became obsolete in 1947.

Left: *The beautiful Imperial Order of the Crown of India. The Badge of this rare award was to be returned upon the death of the holder – as is common with most British Orders at their higher grades – and examples are rarely seen.*

Queen Alexandra, consort of King Edward VII. She wears the Royal Family Order of King Edward VII, the Royal Order of Victoria and Albert and the Imperial Order of the Crown of India.

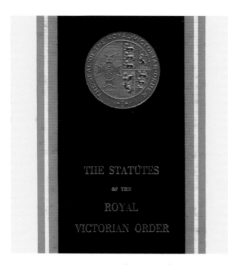

The Statutes of the Royal Victorian Order. The Statutes of an Order contain its current regulations and procedures and may be amended from time to time, as circumstances require.

The Royal Victorian Order (1896)

The last Order to be created during the nineteenth century, this was instituted by Queen Victoria at a time when the award of Orders and other Decorations was increasingly being taken over by the Prime Minister and government of the day.

The Queen wanted an award that could be removed from the control of politicians and the Royal Victorian Order (RVO) remains exclusively in the gift of the monarch, generally conferred for service to the royal family. The Order now has five classes: Knight or Dame Grand Cross (GCVO); Knight or Dame Commander (KCVO/DCVO); Commander (CVO); Lieutenant (LVO); and Member (MVO). They may be conferred on men and women, civil and military, though women were not admitted until 1936. As with most British Orders, Badges are returnable on promotion. The Chapel of the Order is St George's Chapel, Windsor.

Associated with this Order, as a lower tier, is the Royal Victorian Medal (RVM). Originally awarded in silver and bronze but extended during the reign of George V to silver-gilt, silver and bronze, RVMs are given to those below Officer rank for services to the royal family. They are commonly awarded, for example, to the domestic and personal staff of the royal household or for services on royal occasions

The Collar Chain and Badge of the Grand Cross of the Royal Victorian Order. The Collar has alternating octagons and decorative panels in silver-gilt, linked by gold. The octagons have a jewelled gold rose on blue enamel, while the frames contain letters spelling out the formal titles of Queen Victoria, 'VICTORIA BRITT. REG. DEF. FID. IND. IMP.', in white enamel. The Badge is suspended from a central medallion with the Queen's profile in gold and enamels.

Left: *The Sash Badge of the Grand Cross of the Royal Victorian Order. The Badge bears simply the royal cypher of Queen Victoria and the word 'Victoria'.*

Right: *The Breast Star of a Knight or Dame Commander of the Royal Victorian Order. The reverses are individually numbered, but are otherwise plain apart from the pin fastening. The central cross is not enamelled.*

Above: *The Breast Star of the Grand Cross of the Royal Victorian Order.*

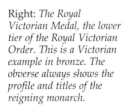

Right: *The Royal Victorian Medal, the lower tier of the Royal Victorian Order. This is a Victorian example in bronze. The obverse always shows the profile and titles of the reigning monarch.*

The reverse of the Breast Badge of a Member of the Royal Victorian Order, showing its identifying number 1089.

The reverse of the bronze Royal Victorian Medal – the lowest grade of the award – with the monogram of Queen Victoria. The reverse always bears the monogram of the reigning monarch.

Right: *The obverse of the MVO. This is a pre-1988 award; in that year, the grades Member Fourth Class (whose Badge is shown here) and Member Fifth Class (whose Badge had frosted silver arms with an enamel central roundel) became Lieutenant (LVO) and Member (MVO) respectively.*

such as state visits or state funerals. Since 1951, foreign recipients of these medals have worn the ribbon with a white stripe down the middle.

The Royal Victorian Chain (1902)

Despite its similarity to the Royal Victorian Order, this Chain is a separate and exclusive award. It was inaugurated in 1902 by Edward VII, a monarch who took a close interest in honours and decorations. It is awarded only to foreign monarchs, princes and heads of state, to very high-ranking members of the royal household and a select few public servants, such as the Archbishops of Canterbury on retirement.

The Royal Victorian Chain. These very select awards are often conferred upon important public figures, such as Archbishops of Canterbury, on their retirement.

The Chain alternates three Tudor roses, two thistles, two shamrocks and two lotus flowers in gold, linked with gold chain, with the sovereign's cypher forming the central medallion. From this hangs the Badge, which is essentially that of the Grand Cross of the Royal Victorian Order.

The Chain is worn around the shoulders by men; female recipients wear a bow of ribbon of the Royal Victorian Order, to which are attached single elements of the Chain – an unusual expedient. In 2003 there were fewer than twenty holders, including the Queen, of this rare award.

A group comprising the Member's Badges of the Royal Victorian Order (MVO) and the Order of the British Empire (MBE, first type, Civil Division), with medals for 1914–18; awarded to Captain A. Batty, Indian Army. The MVO was conferred for service during the Prince of Wales's visit to India in 1921–2.

Other Orders
and related awards

The Royal Guelphic Order (1815)

The 1701 Act of Settlement conferred the British crown upon George, 'Elector' of the German state of Hanover. From the beginning of his reign as George I in 1714 until the end of the reign of William IV in 1837 the 'Hanoverian dynasty' also ruled Hanover. The Royal Guelphic Order of Hanover, which had Civil and

Part of the Collar Chain of the Royal Guelphic Order, featuring alternate lions and crowns and the royal cypher of King George III, all in gold.

Military classes in three grades – Knight Grand Cross, Knight Commander and Knight – was instituted in 1815 by the Prince Regent, later King George IV. It took its name and its motto (*Nec aspera terrent*, 'Difficulties do not terrify') from the Guelphs, the royal house of Hanover. The Order was essentially intended to reward the monarch's German subjects but many were conferred upon British citizens for services to Hanover, for example awards to British officers serving with Hanoverian forces during the Napoleonic Wars.

Britain's link with Hanover was severed in 1837 when Queen Victoria ascended the throne, since the Salic law stipulated that no

The Breast Star of the Grand Cross of the Guelphic Order of Hanover. This Order had Military and Civil Divisions, distinguished (as was common in many European Orders) by the inclusion of crossed swords through the centre of the device for military recipients.

The Breast Badge of a Knight Commander of the Royal Guelphic Order, Military Division.

woman could become ruler of the state. The Queen's uncle, the Duke of Cumberland, acceded to the throne of Hanover and thereafter the Guelphic Order became a purely Hanoverian and German award.

The Distinguished Service Order (1886)

As Britain's empire expanded during the nineteenth century, it was felt that no means existed of rewarding distinguished service by military and naval officers on campaign. Although they were eligible for existing Orders, these were seldom conferred upon junior officers or awarded simply for campaign service. Likewise, the Victoria Cross, instituted in 1856, was intended only for conspicuous gallantry in action and did not answer the requirement for an immediate award for officers.

One earlier attempt to alleviate this problem had been the creation of the Companion level (CB) of the Order of the Bath in 1815. However, as the century progressed, the CB became more of a senior officers' long-service award, often conferred on retirement or at least for service over a longer period than a single campaign.

In 1886, the Distinguished Service Order (DSO) was instituted by Royal Warrant to provide an immediate reward for military and naval officers of lower rank who had 'distinguished' themselves on campaign. The first were awarded for the conquest of Burma, 1885–7, and for actions on the Egypt–Sudan border.

Although originally intended to reward service on campaign, the DSO was later granted for meritorious and non-combatant service. This caused such contention in the First World War that it was decreed in January 1917 that the Order should be granted only to the 'fighting services', the implication being that it was to reward service 'before the enemy' rather than work behind the lines. The DSO was opened to the

The Distinguished Service Order: the Breast Badge of this single-class military award, with the cypher of Queen Victoria. This is an early example in gold, worn with the medal for Egypt and the Sudan, 1882–8. The Badge was produced in silver-gilt after 1889.

Far left: *The Distinguished Service Order: the reverse of the George V type as awarded during the First World War. From 1938 the date of award has been engraved on the reverse of the lower arm. The monarch's cypher in the centre ('GRI' in this case) varies from reign to reign.*

Left: *The standard obverse of the Distinguished Service Order, which has not changed since its inception in 1886. Since 1993 this Order has been open to all ranks, not just to officers, for qualities of leadership on campaign.*

Royal Air Force in 1918 and to the Merchant Navy, Home Guard and other services in 1942.

As a result of John Major's 1993 reorganisation of the honours system along more egalitarian lines, the DSO's availability has been widened to include all ranks and it is awarded only for leadership, not for gallantry. The first such appointments were made for service in operations in 'former Yugoslavia', including Bosnia.

Although recipients are 'appointed' to the DSO, it is in many ways an atypical Order as it has only one class (and that restricted to the military) and confers no title or status in itself; there was considerable criticism of the title of the award when it was instituted in 1886. It is better considered as a Decoration – a military award for gallantry or leadership – rather than as a true Order.

The Distinguished Service Order with second award bar – indicating two awards of the decoration – in a group which includes the Military Cross, three medals for 1914–18 and two for 1939–45.

The Order of British India: (below) First Class Badge, pattern of 1938–47; (right) Second Class Badge. The First Class is slightly larger and has a crown above the central roundel. The reverse is plain and slightly convex. The original ribbon was light blue, altered to plain crimson in 1838. Stripes were added in 1939 – two thin blue stripes for the First Class and a single blue stripe for the Second.

The Order of British India (1837)

Instituted on 17th April 1837 by the East India Company, this Order rewarded 'long, faithful and honourable' service by native officers of the Company's Indian Army and continued in use when the Company's powers were removed after the Indian Mutiny. There were two classes, the gold and enamel Badges being worn around the neck, and the award entitled the recipient to the post-nominal title *Bahadur* ('Hero') for the Second Class and *Sardar Bahadur* ('Heroic Leader') for the First Class. It was accompanied by increased pay and pension allowances.

Although there are instances of this highly regarded Order being granted for distinguished service on a particular campaign, the OBI was generally given to long-serving Indian officers (between twenty and thirty years' service was common) who had rendered meritorious service.

The Order became obsolete in 1947 when India achieved independence.

The Order of Burma (1940)

This rare gold award was instituted by George VI in 1940, after Burma had been separated from the Indian Empire for

The gold Neck Badge of the Order of Burma. The central medallion bearing the peacock device is in blue enamel; the ribbon is dark green with edge-stripes of light blue.

administrative purposes. It was intended to reward native officers of the Burmese army in the same way as the Order of British India did for the Indian Army, and was worn around the neck from a ribbon of dark green with light blue edges. After 1945 the Order was conferred for distinguished service or for gallantry as much as for long service, but as only twenty-four were ever granted they are seldom seen.

The Order became obsolete in 1947 when Burma became independent.

The *Kaisar-i-Hind* Medal (1900)

The *Kaisar-i-Hind* ('Emperor of India') Medal was instituted in May 1900 to reward public service in India – for example, in social work, education or medical aid – and was awarded regardless of race, religion or sex. It was initially instituted in two classes (the First Class in gold and the Second Class in silver), but a Third Class in bronze was added during the reign of George V and the Medals were reduced slightly in size. Early issues are solid, later ones hollow. Decorative dated bars, borne on the ribbon, could be granted to reward further services. Each Medal bore on the obverse the intertwined monogram of the monarch and on the reverse the legend 'For Public Service in

Far left: *The Kaisar-i-Hind Medal in gold, with the monogram of Queen Victoria.*

Left: *The Kaisar-i-Hind Medal in gold, with the monogram of King George V and decorative wearing-brooch, integral to the award. The silver and bronze awards were identical in design.*

The Indian Order of Merit, 1837–1947. Shown here is the Third Class (1837–1911), in silver and enamel. The Second Class was silver with a gold central wreath, while the First Class, of which only forty-two were awarded, was entirely in gold with an enamel centre. All classes were worn as Breast Badges.

India', in a band around a floral spray. As was usual, ladies wore the Medal on a bow of the ribbon, which was a plain bluish green.

Like the other British-Indian awards, the *Kaisar-i-Hind* Medal became obsolete in 1947 when India gained its independence.

The Indian Order of Merit (1837)

Essentially a gallantry award, the Indian Order of Merit was instituted in three classes by the East India Company in 1837, along with the Order of British India, and remained the only gallantry award for native soldiers of the Indian Army until the introduction of the Indian Distinguished Service Medal in 1907 and the extension of the Victoria Cross to Indian soldiers in 1911. At that point the Order was reduced to two classes, the Victoria Cross being deemed to have replaced the First Class, and it was reduced to one class in 1944.

The Indian Order of Merit, Third Class, along with a campaign Medal for the North West Frontier of India, 1895–1902, and the 1911 Coronation (Delhi Durbar) Medal for India.

The Indian Order of Merit, Second Class, 1939–45. The central wording was altered from 'Reward of Valor' to 'Reward of Gallantry' in 1939 and the Order was reduced to one class in 1944.

A Civil version in two classes was instituted in 1902 and reduced to one class in 1939, but was rarely awarded.

Technically, a recipient had to be in possession of one class before he could be advanced to a higher grade, but there are instances of soldiers being appointed straight into the Second or First Class (for example during the Indian Mutiny of 1857–8), their repeated gallantry in action being deemed to have earned them the lower class, even if it was not physically awarded. The Order carried increased pay and pension allowances (payable to the widow if the soldier was killed) and was very highly regarded.

Both Military and Civil Divisions became obsolete when India became independent in 1947.

The Royal Red Cross (1883)

This award was instituted in 1883 as a single-class Decoration and was extended to two classes in 1915 when the circumstances of the First World War called for a more widely available reward. Its classes thereafter were First Class or 'Member' (RRC) and Second Class or 'Associate' (ARRC).

The Royal Red Cross was intended to reward the military nursing services for zeal in attending sick and wounded servicemen and was unusual in that it was initially conferred only upon women – a situation not altered until 1976, when male members of the nursing services became eligible. Recipients have to be in possession of the Second Class before they can be promoted into the First Class, after which further awards take the form of silver bars, introduced in 1917 and worn on the ribbon of the First Class. Foreign and non-military recipients may be awarded the Decoration as honorary members.

The Imperial Service Order (1902)

This was another of the awards instituted by Edward VII and was intended to reward long service in the senior echelons of the Civil Service

The Order of the Royal Red Cross: in gold, with the profile of Queen Victoria. The Badge was produced in silver-gilt from 1889. The Second Class, introduced in 1915, is in frosted silver and enamel.

The Victorian Royal Red Cross, worn with the Medal for South Africa, 1877–9. The Order was intended to reward the services of military nurses and could, as here, be awarded for duties on campaign.

Right: *The Royal Red Cross, First Class with bar, with George V obverse. This shows the typical 'ribbon bow' arrangement from which the Neck Badges of most Orders are worn by ladies.*

and administrative departments of central, local and overseas government. Unusually, the design of the Badge varies for men and women, the latter being admitted to the Order from 1908. That for men is star-shaped, while that for women is round with its design edged by a wreath of laurels.

Although designated an Order, the Imperial Service Order (ISO) had only one class and is really a 'long service and good conduct'

The Imperial Service Order, Gentleman's Badge, with the monogram of Elizabeth II. The reverse is plain except for the name of the recipient. The central medallion is in gold for the ISO (as here) and in silver for the first-type Imperial Service Medal.

Above: *A cased Imperial Service Medal, first type, pre-1920, with cypher of George V. It is identical to the Badge of the Imperial Service Order except that its centre is in silver. The ladies' version was circular, not star-shaped.*

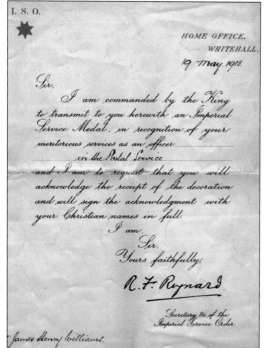

A document notifying the award of the Imperial Service Medal in 1913, 'in recognition of meritorious service as an officer in the Postal Services'.

The reverse of the Imperial Service Medal. The obverse bears the usual effigy and titles of the reigning monarch. The award was reduced to a standard circular silver Medal in 1920, although it is slightly smaller than most other British medals.

award. In the United Kingdom, service of twenty-five years was the requirement, with twenty years and six months in India and sixteen years in the tropics. Service of an exceptionally meritorious nature could, however, lead to the award of the ISO without the usual length of service being fulfilled.

The Order was sparingly granted, with slightly more than two thousand conferred upon men and only 127 upon ladies. No awards have been made since 1995, when the ISO became another victim of the 1993 revision of the honours system.

Associated with the ISO since its foundation is the *Imperial Service Medal* (ISM) – a lower-tier award intended for the junior grades of the Civil Service and related bodies. The original Medal was similar in shape and size to the Badge of the ISO, but with its central medallion in silver, not gold. In 1920 it was altered to a circular silver Medal bearing the reigning sovereign's current effigy and titles on the obverse and an allegorical scene on the reverse, depicting a naked man resting from his labours, above the words 'For Faithful Service'. Unlike the Order, the ISM has not fallen victim to the restructuring of 1993.

The Order of St John of Jerusalem (1888)

The ancient Order of St John of Jerusalem, dating back to the Crusades, was proscribed in England during the Reformation under Henry VIII. In the 1820s moves were made to re-establish an 'English tongue' of what was then an essentially Catholic Order, but when these failed an independent English 'Sovereign and Illustrious Order of St John of Jerusalem, Anglia' was established instead. This was an unofficial Order with no connection to the continental Order of St John or to the British Crown. However, as a result of its charitable work the Order was granted a Royal Charter on 4th May 1888, Queen Victoria becoming its Sovereign Head.

The Breast Star and Neck Badge of a Knight or Dame of Grace of the Order of St John of Jerusalem. The badges at this level are in silver and white enamel, with silver lions and unicorns at the intersection of the arms of the cross. The ribbons of all awards are plain black.

Insignia of a Knight or Dame of Justice of the Order of St John, c.1880. Note the additional crown suspension to the Neck Badge. The Badges at this level are in gold and white enamel, without lions and unicorns at the intersection of the arms of the cross.

It is unique as a British Order in that it is not conferred by the monarch, but under the monarch's authority by a private body. It is essentially a 'society' award of what is now known as 'The Grand Priory of the Most Venerable Order of the Hospital of St John of Jerusalem'.

The monarch is Sovereign Head and Patron of the Order, under whom is the Grand Prior. The six classes of the Order are: Bailiff or Dame Grand Cross; Knight or Dame of Justice; Knight or Dame of Grace; Commander; Officer; and Serving Brother or Sister. In addition, 'Associate' status (restyled 'Member' in 1999) may be conferred upon non-Christian appointees or those who are not citizens of the United Kingdom, the Irish Republic or the Commonwealth; they initially rank as Serving Brother or Sister but may be promoted to any grade for further services. 'Donat' status may be conferred upon those who have made contributions to the funds of the Order.

The Order of St John is well known for its hospital, first-aid and ambulance services and for its teaching work in those areas. Members of the various grades of the Order, with its distinctive plain black ribbon and the familiar silver or white Maltese Cross emblem that is the basis of its insignia, wear the Neck Badges, Breast Stars and Breast Badges in similar fashion to those of other British Orders. The society also confers a separate range of life-saving and long-service awards.

The Order of the League of Mercy (1898/1999)

The League of Mercy was founded in 1898 and received a Royal Charter in 1899. It was a charitable organisation whose members did voluntary work in hospitals, with the poor or in other areas of relief work. The Order ceased to function in 1947, when its Royal Charter was withdrawn at the time of the founding of the National Health Service, but it was re-established in March 1999.

The pre-1947 Badge was a red enamelled cross suspended from the Three Feathers device of the Prince of Wales; the central roundel depicted the figure of Charity tending the poor. The reverse was plain, except for the title of the Order and date of foundation; they

First Badge of the Order of the League of Mercy, a charitable institution which between 1898 and 1947 conferred these awards for voluntary service in charitable work. The new badge does not bear the emblem of the Prince of Wales.

The reverse of the pre-1947 Badge of the Order of the League of Mercy, showing the date of the Order's foundation. They are sometimes found named on the reverse. The new badge has '1999' in place of '1898'.

are sometimes found engraved with the recipient's name. The 1999 Badge is essentially the same, but without enamel, the cross and central device being plain silver gilt; the date on the reverse has been altered to '1999'. The ribbon is the same for both issues: white with a broad central dark blue stripe.

The pre-1947 cross was awarded for five years' voluntary charitable work while the present award may be conferred for a minimum of seven years' work with the sick, the disabled or the disadvantaged.

Medal group with the Distinguished Service Order (DSO) and the Member's Badge of the Royal Victorian Order (MVO), worn with an array of campaign medals for the First World War, the North West Frontier of India, the Second World War and the Coronation in India (Delhi Durbar), 1911.

Abbreviations

Below are the standard post-nominal abbreviations used by recipients of the various Orders and related awards.

ARRC	Associate (i.e. Second Class) of the Royal Red Cross
BEM	British Empire Medal
CB	Companion of the Order of the Bath
CBE	Commander of the Order of the British Empire
CH	Companion of Honour
CI	Imperial Order of the Crown of India
CIE	Companion of the Order of the Indian Empire
CMG	Companion of the Order of St Michael and St George
CSI	Companion of the Order of the Star of India
CVO	Commander of the Royal Victorian Order
DBE	Dame Commander of the Order of the British Empire
DCB	Dame Commander of the Order of the Bath
DCMG	Dame Commander of the Order of St Michael and St George
DCVO	Dame Commander of the Royal Victorian Order
DSO	Distinguished Service Order
EGM	Empire Gallantry Medal
GBE	Knight or Dame Grand Cross of the Order of the British Empire
GCB	Knight or Dame Grand Cross of the Order of the Bath
GCH	Knight Grand Cross of the Royal Guelphic Order
GCIE	Knight Grand Commander of the Order of the Indian Empire
GCMG	Knight or Dame Grand Cross of the Order of St Michael and St George
GCSI	Knight Grand Commander of the Order of the Star of India
GCVO	Knight or Dame Grand Cross of the Royal Victorian Order
IOM	Indian Order of Merit
ISM	Imperial Service Medal
ISO	Imperial Service Order
KB	Knight Bachelor or Knight of the Order of the Bath
KBE	Knight Commander of the Order of the British Empire
KCB	Knight Commander of the Order of the Bath
KCH	Knight Commander of the Royal Guelphic Order
KCIE	Knight Commander of the Order of the Indian Empire
KCMG	Knight Commander of the Order of St Michael and St George
KCSI	Knight Commander of the Order of the Star of India
KCVO	Knight Commander of the Royal Victorian Order
KG	Knight of the Order of the Garter
KH	Knight of the Royal Guelphic Order
KP	Knight of the Order of St Patrick
KT	Knight of the Order of the Thistle
LG	Lady of the Order of the Garter
LT	Lady of the Order of the Thistle
LVO	Lieutenant of the Royal Victorian Order
MBE	Member of the Order of the British Empire
MVO	Member of the Royal Victorian Order
OB	Order of Burma
OBE	Officer of the Order of the British Empire
OBI	Order of British India
OM	Order of Merit
RRC	Member (i.e. First Class) of the Royal Red Cross
RVM	Royal Victorian Medal

Further reading

Interest in the older Orders has been such that reference works on some can be found that date back to the late seventeenth century, an example being *The Institution, Laws and Ceremonies of the Most Noble Order of the Garter*, published in 1672 by Elias Ashmole. Such publications, however, are now rare collectors' items in their own right. Those listed below represent some of the modern sources that can be consulted for a detailed history and description of the various awards.

The leading society for the study of Orders, Decorations and Medals is *The Orders and Medals Research Society*, which publishes a regular journal. The membership secretary's address is: PO Box 248, Snettisham, King's Lynn, Norfolk PE31 7TA; the society's website is at www.omrs.org.uk

Past copies of *The London Gazette*, which announces appointments to an Order, are often available in major city libraries, in the National Archives, Ruskin Avenue, Kew, Richmond, Surrey TW9 4DU, or (in the case of more recent editions) on the Internet at www.london-gazette.co.uk

Begent, P. J., and Chesshyre, H. *The Most Noble Order of the Garter, 650 Years*. Spink & Son, 1999.
de la Bere, Sir Ivan. *The Queen's Orders of Chivalry*. William Kimber, 1961.
Fellowes, E. H. *The Knights of the Garter 1348–1939*. Oxford University Press, 1939.
Galloway, P. *The Most Illustrious Order* [St Patrick]. Unicorn Press, 1983.
Galloway, P. *The Order of the British Empire*. Spink & Son, 1996.
Galloway, P. *The Order of St Michael and St George*. Spink & Son, 2000.
Galloway, P., and Martin, S. *Royal Service* (two volumes). Spink & Son, 1996–2001.
HMSO. *Aspects of Britain: Honours and Titles*. 1996.
Innes, Sir T. *The Foundation of the Most Ancient and Most Noble Order of the Thistle*. Edinburgh, 1959.
Patterson, S. *Royal Insignia*. Merrell, 1996.
Risk, J. C. *The History of the Order of the Bath and Its Insignia*. Spink & Son, 1982.
The Statutes of the various Orders.
Tozer, C. W. *The Insignia and Medals of the Grand Priory of the Most Venerable Order of St John of Jerusalem*. Hayward, 1975.
Vickers, H. *Royal Orders: The Honours and the Honoured*. Boxtree, 1994.

Websites
The Internet provides a wealth of sites that illustrate and describe British Orders. Sites particularly worth consulting are: *The Monarchy Today* (www.royal.gov.uk); *The British Orders of Chivalry* (www.kwtelecom.com/chivalry/britords) and the Cabinet Office site (www.cabinet-office.gov.uk). However, any Internet search for one or other of the British Orders is likely to produce a range of useful and informative sites.

Some leading dealers and auctioneers
(These issue regular sales or auction lists to subscribers or attend weekend fairs.)
Andrew Bostock, 15 Waller Close, Leek Wootton, Warwickshire CV35 7QG. Telephone/fax: 01926 856381.
Philip Burman, The Cottage, Blackborough End, Middleton, King's Lynn, Norfolk PE32 1SE. Telephone: 01553 840350. Website: www.military-medals.co.uk
Peter Cotrel, 7 Stanton Road, Bournemouth, Dorset BH10 5DS. Telephone/fax: 01202 388367; mobile: 07971 019155.
C. J. and A. J. Dixon, First Floor, 23 Prospect Street, Bridlington, East Yorkshire YO15 2AE. Telephone: 01262 603348 or 676877. Website: www.dixonsmedals.com
DNW, 16 Bolton Street, London W1J 8BQ. Telephone: 020 7016 1700. Website: www.DNW.co.uk
Spink & Son, 69 Southampton Row, Bloomsbury, London WC1B 4ET. Telephone: 020 7563 4000. Website: www.spink-online.com

---

Places to visit

There are over 150 local regimental and military museums in the United Kingdom which have collections of Orders, Decorations and Medals. Readers should consult the current edition of *A Guide to Military Museums* by T. and S. Wise (Imperial Press) for information on the location, content and opening hours of these museums. Some stately homes and country houses (whose details can be found in various guides and handbooks) contain fine collections of Decorations as part of their displays of family history – for example, Apsley House in London displays the Orders, Decorations and Medals of the Duke of Wellington, Chartwell in Kent has the awards of Sir Winston Churchill, and the National Trust properties Plas Newydd and Powis Castle in Wales have good collections of family awards.
    Collections of Orders and related Decorations are best seen in major military museums; the main ones are listed below.

The Imperial War Museum, Lambeth Road, London SE1 6HZ. Telephone: 020 7416 5320. Website: www.iwm.org.uk
The National Army Museum, Royal Hospital Road, Chelsea, London SW3 4HT. Telephone: 020 7730 0717. Website: national-army-museum.ac.uk
The Royal Air Force Museum, Grahame Park Way, Hendon, London NW9 5LL. Telephone: 020 8205 2266. Website: www.rafmuseum.org.uk
The Royal Naval Museum, HM Naval Base, Portsmouth, Hampshire PO1 3NH. Telephone: 023 9272 7562. Website: www.royalnavalmuseum.org

Index